MW00891579

Copyright

<u>DISCLAIMER</u>

This work is an unofficial summary of the original book, *The Energy Paradox: When Your Get-Up-And-Go Has Got Up and Gone* by Steven Gundry. It is written to capture the key points in the book and help the reader understand the main gist of the author. It features discussion questions, cover questions, and background information segments, making it an effective study material. Also, note that the content in this material isn't intended to replace the need for seeking independent professional help or advice when appropriate.

Just a Moment!

Download Your Free GIFT!

Just before you proceed, we have a valuable GIFT for you FREE of charge. Simply click HERE to get yours as soon as possible!

Alternatively, you can scan the QR code to access the download page

Table of Content

Background Information about the Author, Steven R. Gundry

Steven R Gundry is an American physician and health author. He specializes in the fields of cardiothoracic surgery and nutrition. He trained as a physician at the Medical College of Georgia, from which he graduated in 1977. He is recognized as a pioneer in Infant Cardiothoracic surgery after his successful surgery, in conjunction with Dr. Leonard Bailey, on an Infant's mitral verve. Steven Gundry is popularly known for his controversial book, *The Plant Paradox* (2017). He is also the author of *Dr. Gundry's Diet Evolution: Turn Off the Genes That Are Killing You and Your Waistline* (2008) and, of course, *The Energy Paradox: When Your Get-Up-And-Go Has Got Up and Gone* (2021).

Summary Overview of *The Energy Paradox: When Your Get-Up-And-Go Has Got Up and Gone* by Steven Gundry

The Energy Paradox is a medical self-help book by Steven R. Gundry, which seeks to educate you on the basic ways of addressing your energy crises. The book reveals the several often-ignored factors in diet, lifestyle, and occasional practices which pose a threat to one's energy and overall health by causing inflammation, insulin resistance, etc. To effectively address these factors towards energy production and overall health, Gundry prescribes proven guidelines for improving our diet and lifestyle. The book also features *The Energy Paradox Program,* which provides precise blueprints for transforming your energy life and overall health most comfortably and effectively.

Introduction: I Just Trust You Don't Have It in Me

The author, Steven R. Gundry, narrates how he was inspired to write this book. Once, on his way to a TV studio where he was supposed to be interviewed on-air for a fundraising program, he received a call from the producer who tells him that the program presenter wouldn't be able to make it. Upon inquiring the cause of her unavailability, he learned she's been feeling like her energy was evaporating, and this feeling was at its peak that day.

Gundry explains that he has experienced several patients who express that they are suffering from one form of fatigue or another. Also, as a restorative medicine physician, he has had around 70 percent of the patients in his *Centers for Restorative Medicine in Santa Barbara and Palm Springs*, California, come to be treated for autoimmune conditions, which are naturally very exhausting. By addressing the diseases or conditions in themselves (being the sources of the fatigues), he has recorded multiple successes in helping patients regain energy. This springs from the fact that *energy comes back*. However, the phone call about the TV presenter, Lathy, forced him to think more about energy and how it can be lost.

In his investigations, Gundry discovered that everyone, to some degree, experience one form of energy loss or another. But this excludes sleep deprivation, physical exhaustion (which we may experience after a prolonged period of hard work), etc. Also, it doesn't include chronic fatigue syndrome, POTS (postural orthostatic tachycardia syndrome), or other underlying illnesses. He maintains that the kind of tiredness (or fatigue) addressed here is that which drains someone of their usual energy, capacity, or clarity, within the context of their normal life. It is an inertia that is experienced by those who we may call the "unsick."

Gundry began noticing energy problems first in patients who came to see him for general maintenance. These were men and women who were doing well by general assessment and who don't have diagnosed conditions. Yet, a great number of them admit that they are constantly getting fatigued. This category cuts across the board and doesn't necessarily conform to our stereotypes. They include young children, parents, busy entrepreneurs, etc. This phenomenon is growing in scope and particularly prevalent in our society. This is evident in the several canceled dinners, calling off play dates, discussions about fatigue, etc.

Gundry maintains that the reason why you feel you "don't have it in you" (fatigue) is because you actually don't. This largely owes to the fact that our modern lifestyle (movement, nutrition, sleeping patterns) depletes rather than restore. Consequently, the "tank" of one's energy is constantly being depleted without being properly refueled.

Gundry states that this book is written to inform the reader that fatigue is a physiological state that features one's overall health. This is based on the fact that energy keeps one alive since it is responsible for keeping every organ of the body (including the brain) alive. This book seeks to educate the reader that they can have more control over their energy than they think. It seeks to do this based on the understanding of three root principles behind energy production. They are:

- **Overfed but Underpowered**: This is comparable to having more fuel access but feeling out of gas. This is because of the food we eat in modern times: even though they taste normal, they have lesser nutrients than that which was available to our grandparents. The cause of this and how to deal with it is addressed in chapter 2.

- **E=M2C2:** This is an Einstein-inspired formula. However, in this context, it illustrates how energy is maximized. M2 stands for *microbiome* (the group of helpful bacteria in the intestines or gut) and *mitochondria* (the organelles in the cell that turns nutrients from oxygen and food into energy). The C2 stands for *Chrono consumption*, which describes time-controlled eating. Eating the right food at the right time empowers the microbiome and mitochondria to heal and regenerate. This is discussed in chapter 3.

- **Postbiotics (Not probiotics or prebiotics):** Postbiotics refer to the compounds through which the gut microbiome and the mitochondria communicate. They constitute a newly-discovered system that aids the communication between the gut microbiome and the mitochondria. This communication is constantly under strain from improper nutrition and harmful chemicals.

By attending to each part of the formula (the Ms and Cs) without overwhelming your system, you can turn your energy around. This book presents a program that is most effective for doing this. This is broken down into parts and chapters in this book.

Part 1: The Epidemic of Fatigue

Chapter 1: How Did We Get Here?

Over time, we have tried to live with our being tired. Given our incredible nature and hard will, we can adapt to changes and keep going when fatigue sets in. This explains why we opt for caffeine, sugar, and other energy-boosting supplements. We tend to treat this fatigue as a natural phenomenon we can just deal with. However, contrary to this perspective, Gundry maintains that any fatigue we can't just shake off is neither natural nor an expected sign of aging (contrary to the assumption of many). Also, just because one can push through fatigue doesn't make it normal.

In his over twenty years of practice in restorative medicine, Gundry maintains that he has observed that only in rare cases were fatigue-related symptoms linked to life-altering illnesses. Most people who experience it have no significant illness and tend to only show up for medical checkups. However, it always turns out that this second group showed identifiable markers of ill health in their blood similar to that found in the first group (those with significant illnesses).

Gundry maintains that there is a glaring paradox in the core of health and disease (in the context of energy). This paradox is that when we are eating more energy-rich foods, we're more deprived of energy. Similarly, with our less physically demanding lifestyle than that of our forbearers, we feel more physically exhausted.

Traditional medicine has been unable to capture this reality. This is because it doesn't fit into the conventional medicine system: the fact that it can't be measured, tracked like blood pressure or cholesterol level makes this evident. Also, the fact that there is no pill to address it makes it mostly avoided modern medicine. Some physicians may even be tempted to assume that the phenomenon of energy loss is imagined. Physicians are only willing to treat a situation they believe is bad enough to warrant medication.

Besides the fact that fatigue doesn't get the attention of conventional medicine, we live in an age of high competition is another reason it doesn't get the right attention in our society.

We tend to shelve our feeling of fatigue when we see that everyone else seems to be bursting with life on social media.

Against the generally dismissive attitude towards tiredness, Gundry argues that it is not imagined. Even though it may end in the head (with symptoms like brain fog, low mood, etc.), it originally starts in the gut. Gut-derived inflammation and changes in the *microbiome* are particularly responsible for this subclinical state (constant fatigue or exhaustion). Gundry expression of this state as when your get-up-and-go has got up and gone (or GUAG, for short).

The GUAG phenomenon, although overlooked, is probably the biggest health complaint of recent times. The stats support this. A recent survey showed that over half of American adults never feel well-rested through the week. However, the subject of stress has attracted more data gathering than fatigue. Nevertheless, both stress and fatigue have a lot in common. This is because they often exist together. Yet, the fact remains that stress or burnout gets more attention than fatigue. This owes in part to the economic consequences of stress on American workers. A recent survey shows that almost a quarter of employees reported being burned out often, and forty-four percent claimed to be burned out sometimes.

Fatigue and stress have a large ripple effect, despite sounding harmless. This is the fact that tired and stressed humans are likely to make poor food and lifestyle choices. These compound their fatigue. Sources of fatigue include not eating food that supports their energy-producing mitochondria and feeding on processed foods that starve their gut microbiome. They also tend to stay away from exercises while also altering their natural sleep cycle by using their mobile devices. The more exhausted we are, the poorer our choices.

Many have subscribed to the use of caffeine, energy drinks, and the likes to boost our energy to deal with fatigue. While these may not be inherently bad, using them only masks the underlying issue and doesn't solve it.

A Global Quest for Energy

In his research into how energy is lost, Gundry examines the health of the Hadza people, some of the last set of hunter-gatherers in the savannah-woodlands of Tanzania. Their way of life has been critically studied for its similarities to that of Pleistocene ancestors. They hunt for food using primitive tools like bows, arrows, etc. Their men walk six to ten miles daily hunting for games, and their women walk three and a half miles gathering plant foods. An astounding feature of the Hadza people is their high level of physical exertion and overall fitness.

Now, quite surprisingly, research has shown that the Hadza's expended almost the same energy as modern-day desk workers. This leads one to question where most of the energy expended by these desk workers goes. Based on this discovery, Gundry concludes that something was responsible for the unexplained energy exertion in the sedentary desk workers, making them spend almost as much energy as the physically active Hadzas. This, for him, owes to the variations in diet and lifestyle and lack of exposure to natural forces like the sun.

While the Hadzas feed on organic foods like fiber-rich plants and lean meat, which keeps their body functioning normally, modern Americans have a diet that harms their systems. The Hadzas also avoid the constant energy loss which the modern Western lifestyle results in—inflammation.

In this chapter, Steven Gundy examines inflammation and its roles in the loss of energy. Inflammation is the body's response to a microbe invasion. It is a response of the body's immune system that dates back to millions of years ago, before the emergence of the *Homo Sapiens*. It serves primarily to protect the body from potentially harmful bacteria, viruses, fungi, or molds. It detects them as they get into the body and mounts a defensive attack against them. This defensive attack is what inflammation is. Inflammation can be obvious (i.e., in the case of a swollen sprain ankle). However, we are not aware of most inflammation that takes place in our bodies.

Inflammation is similar to fire. Humans need it to survive. But, when left unchecked, it can harm the body. A regular inflammation—the body's response to infections—is safe; it is chronic inflammation—the response to our modern diet and lifestyle—that is harmful. Chronic inflammation has been linked to virtually all chronic diseases like diabetes, obesity, neurodegeneration, etc. This addresses the sedentary desk workers who expended almost as much energy as the Hadzas (discussed in chapter 1). Inflammation naturally uses a lot of energy. The desk workers likely have most of their energies consumed by inflammation.

Cytokines describe a chemical in the body that mobilizes energy as an inflammatory response. During inflammation, it mobilizes as much energy as needed to help the body's defense forces fight the invader. Hence, during inflammation, less energy is available for use for other things you need to do. It is an overlooked but key suspect in people experiencing constant exhaustion. Basically, when one's body is inflamed, one tends to feel tired.

The Three Ls of Chronic Inflammation

Gundry discusses three factors (3 Ls) responsible for Chronic Inflammation to discuss the sources of inflammation. They are

- Leaky gut
- Lectins, and
- LPSs

Leaky gut describes the weakening of the gut wall's integrity, leading to the creation of microscopic holes in them. It owes to the large amounts of processed foods, harmful plant foods, and chemicals consumed in recent times. Holes in the gut wall cause bacteria and other harmful microbes to leak into the intestines, tissues, and bloodstreams. Now, about seventy to eighty percent of the immune system lives around the gut wall tissues. Hence, once there is a leaky gut, there'll definitely be inflammation.

Lectins are the proteins in certain plants which serve to protect their seeds from being eaten by predators. An example of lectins is gluten. There are several others found in grains, legumes, vegetables, milk, fruits, etc. Most of our modern diet contains lectins. They can be hard to avoid. Now, lectins naturally attack the gut wall, causing holes in it while also irritating it. This way, they cause inflammation there.

LPSs represent a short form of lipopolysaccharides. They are pieces of bacterial cell walls that can trigger inflammation when they pass through the gut wall. LPSs are harmless when contained within the guts. However, when they leak into the bloodstream, they provoke an attack from the immune system, resulting in inflammation. LPS can be transported in the body through the blood and lymph, thus activating the immune system response everywhere, including the brain. LPS can also circulate in the body through fat transport molecules like *chylomicrons*. This has led to an understanding of why the Standard Western is said to be inflammatory.

Your Immune System at Work: Protecting You at All Costs

The immune system is a far-reaching network that extends to the body organs, lymph tissue, lymph fluid, glands, and immune cells (white blood cells). The gut hosts seventy to eighty percent of the immune cells because the intestines are where most potential pathogens invade. Potential pathogens mostly come through the food or liquid consumed. They can also come via other ways, like through the ears, nose, or eyes. In the event of the invasion of a potential pathogen, the body's defense forces scan it through "tiny little radars" or TLRs [a coinage by the author].

TLRs are found in all cell membranes; they scan every protein in their path to ascertain its threat level. When any harmful protein (or pathogen) is found, TLRs stirs white blood cells to invade the enemy pathogen. This results in symptoms like coughing, sneezing, tiredness, etc., when one has the flu, for instance. The body's response against pathogens is likely to last a few days until the pathogens are eliminated.

At this point, *Cytokines* can withdraw the energy directed at the process. Then, normal energy production and distribution can begin, and one can feel normal again. However, if inflammation continues unchecked, it can result in serious problems. A leaky gut, for instance, can culminate in a hyperactivated immune system. This can be responsible for autoimmune disorders. Subsequent chapters examine ways to keep inflammation in check.

A 1936 U.S senate document is quoted to have said, "...fruits, vegetables, and grains—now being raised on millions of acres of land that no longer contains enough of certain needed nutrients, are starving us—no matter how much we eat of them." Based on this quote, Gundry maintains that modern agricultural practices are responsible for the depletion of nutrients in the soil. Given this, the plants we grow in it have become less nutritious.

Like plants have their roots in the soil for the absorption of nutrients, we have a system of "intestinal roots" in our guts which helps to take in nutrients and produce immune responses. However, this system can be easily harmed if it lacks healthy enough "soil" around it. Soil, in this context, refers to the hundreds of trillions of healthy microbes and bacteria around the roots in the gut. They're valuable for one's overall health and energy. Just as the case is with plants, when the gut "roots" aren't properly cared for, overall health may be affected. This shows how humans are dependent on a healthy "soil" to be healthy.

Gut Buddies: Your Soil's Superorganism

In the past, doctors thought the intestinal tract is just a hollow tube that absorbed food and passed out the resultant waster products. However, now, we understand that the gastrointestinal system contains a world of species in the body. These species—microbial organisms—work daily to ensure that their home (the body) is healthy. They comprise trillions of bacteria, yeast, fungi, worms, viruses, and protozoa. They live in all places in the body—your nose, skin, mouth, vaginal canal, or the immediate air space around you (forming a sort of microscopic cloud around your body). Altogether, these species are your holobiome.

Your holobiome weighs about five pounds in total mass. It is a mass of organisms that have DNA distinct from yours but works with your cells and your genes (it's why some call them "virtual organ"). It has been described as a "cloud computer" which sends and receives data about what goes on within and without the body and what is required for survival. It sends messages back to the cells. It is the main subject of your health and energy.

The bacteria is the most recognized of all microbes in the holobiome. There are trillions of them and about ten thousand different species of them alone. About seventy percent of these bacteria live in the intestines. The most recognized of these are those that live in the large intestine or colon. These bugs altogether make up the gut microbiome and are critical to energy production.

The bacteria and fungi in the gut coexist together in a symbiotic relationship. A healthy microbiome would mean that the most beneficial strains (gut buddies) occupy most of the gut wall. When these helpful microbiomes thrive, they help to keep harmful microbes in check. All microbes in the gut have their specific purposes, and none is out to harm their hosts. However, the right order is that the most helpful ones (gut buddies) overwhelm the less helpful ones. This prevents a situation in which the harmful microbes will hijack the gut. For instance, *succinate*, a metabolite produced by helpful microbes, which helps in energy production, can become destructive and cause inflammation when the right balance isn't maintained.

To keep the right balance, you'd have to supply the microbe ecosystem with the required nutrients and protect it from what it doesn't need. The lack of balance of microbes in the gut has increasingly been linked to the collapse of the order in the microbial ecosystem. Just as with other ecosystems in which the collapse of one species poses a threat to survival, a threat to the balance of the microbial ecosystem can have devastating ripple effects. Now, while the Hadzas and other hunter-gatherers have been linked with a balanced microbial ecosystem, the average modern Western person does not. This is because it is raised on processed foods and lacking the fibrous foods it requires to thrive.

Your helpful microbiome (gut buddies) aid in digestion by helping to break down food that the digestive system cannot handle on its own. In addition to this, they help extract energy from food, thus producing vitamins like B12 and folate. They also aid in the production of hormones and help to metabolize the amino acid absorbed from food. Other functions of your gut buddies are the manufacturing of postbiotics (necessary for communication among body systems; improves appetite, mood, hormones, development, etc.)

A balanced microbial ecosystem contributes to the immune system. A diverse gut microbiome contains several strains of bacteria, which are responsible for teaching the immune system to fight off invaders and trust the data sent to it about what goes on outside the body (remember the function of the holobiome as a "cloud computer"). On the contrary, an imbalance in the gut microbiome will block off this communication. When this happens, the TLRs sense the presence of these harmful invaders and ignite an inflammatory response.

When the immune cells spot invaders, they attack them in an attempt to kill them off. In the process of this, they kill some useful cells. This results in a weaker gut, thus causing microbes to escape into surrounding tissues (they make you gain fat when they make it into your fat tissues), liver and heart (thus causing fatty liver), and the brain (resulting in cognitive impairment).

The Fiber Paradox

Our probiotic bacteria (good bacteria) require food. They particularly prefer prebiotic foods. This helps them create a special kind of fatty acid and helps generate gasses that aid communication between the microbiome and cells. These postbiotics, however, depend on prebiotics to prebiotics to produce these compounds.

Fiber is the best source of prebiotic foods. However, it is a nutrient that is underappreciated in American diets. It describes the class of complex carbohydrates that cannot be broken doesn't in the small intestines. They are typically eaten alongside digestible carbohydrates, fats, or proteins. Thus, they help slow the digestion of other foods so that the absorption of simple sugars can be slow enough to help the energy-producing mitochondria absorb relevant nutrients.

Statistics have shown that the diet of the hunter-gatherers consisted of 150 grams of fiber daily, while the modern American diet has only around 20 to 25 grams. The downside of this fact is that the less fiber one eats, the more one becomes sick. This stems from the already-discussed fact that when your gut buddies are starved of the nutrients required, inflammation becomes inevitable.

Now, it is important to avoid whole-grain fibers (bran muffin, bran-fiber cereal, etc.) in going for fiber. This is because they are lectin-filled and can thus have a negative impact. Healthy energy-producing fiber is full of soluble and insoluble fibers from plant tubers, leaves, stems, etc. (sauerkraut, salad, or asparagus) rather than grains. These are the fibers eaten by the gut microbiome. Soluble fibers are those that dissolve in water, and insoluble ones are the ones that don't. Crispy pears, avocadoes, chicory root, onions, leeks, garlic, green bananas, dandelion roots, and asparagus are good sources of soluble prebiotic fibers.

When properly cared for, your gut buddies produce three short-chain fatty acids (SCFAs), of which the most important one is butyrate (which amounts to 10 percent of energy production). The colon cells depend and live on butyrate as their basic energy source. Besides this, butyrate is fundamental to anti-inflammatory hormone production, helps intestinal macrophages avoid mistaking friendly bacteria for enemies, helps regulate cell growth (and prevents them from becoming cancerous). Lack of sufficient SCFAs has been linked to obesity, metabolic syndrome, and bowel diseases.

Many of the cases with fatigue today stem from the fact that they have bombarded their cellular energy system with too much fuel. It is a state in which one is overfed but underpowered, the core puzzle of The Energy Paradox. This owes to a mismatch between the conditions required by the mitochondria and the nutrition they get from us. This entails being denied the nutrition they need to create energy while being overfed with inferior fuel. The resulting mitochondrial malfunction that springs from this is the root of the widespread cases of fatigue that we see today and several cases of diseases like diabetes, heart disease, cardiomyopathies, metabolic syndrome, cancer, autoimmune conditions, etc.

Constant fatigue is a sign that the mitochondria aren't supported or that they may be at risk. This risk means a threat to the cells, tissues, and organs, depriving them of the energy they require. Now, the mitochondria are small; they are tiny organelles in virtually every cell of the body. Some cells can have thousands of mitochondria in them. They are particularly numerous in the liver, heart, brain, and other tissues and organs that live on much energy. They serve the critical purpose of converting regular deposits of foods into energies that the cells can use. Basically, it helps the body meet its regular demand for energy.

Your Mitochondria Are Mighty Flexible

The mitochondria have a double membrane that separates them from other cell components. It also has its DNA (distinct from yours). It can divide its host cell divides; however, it can also divide on its own, independent of cell division (known as *mitogenesis*). They can replicate themselves in the host cell, making it possible for energy production to increase (more mitochondria means more energy). They also contribute to the fate of the cells they inhabit by regulating cellular homeostasis (this includes ensuring communication within the cells and balancing calcium levels). They teach other cell organelles what to do.

The mitochondria are key to producing several steroid hormones like testosterone, estrogen, and sex hormones. It sees the effective transportation of oxygen through the body and ensures adequate blood oxygen levels. This shows that "iron-poor blood" or low hormones can result from troubled mitochondria.

From Flexible to Stuck

The mitochondria energy-making process is known as *cellular respiration*. It is a process that occurs in every single mitochondrion (singular of mitochondria) over several processes. However, it starts with the first phase, in which the food you eat breaks down into carbon molecules that are absorbed into the cells and then into the mitochondria.

The mitochondria then convert these molecules into "electrified particles," after which they are absorbed flow across the inner mitochondrial membrane via some chemical reactions. This causes the particles to get increasingly charged from one level to another. Eventually, each charged oxygen molecule is combined with an enzyme-free positive hydrogen ion to produce a high-energy molecule, Adenosine Triphosphate (ATP).

This energy-production process, like others, produces some by-products like water, carbon dioxide, heat, and pollutants called reactive oxygen species (ROS), which are comparable to vehicle exhaust. ROSs are the causes of oxidative stress when they are more than the body's antioxidant capacity. However, when present in only small measures, they serve as signaling molecules that aid cellular health.

Excessive ROS damages the mitochondria and can culminate in cell death in which the cell explodes (*apoptosis*). This can cause inflammation or alter brain function. How then can one prevent excessive ROS? Thankfully, normal-functioning mitochondria produce enough antioxidants to keep them minimal so that they can serve their positive signaling duties.

In the process in which mitochondria process fuel to produce ATP, fiber plays an important role. Fiber ensures that the absorption and digestion of different food components (carbohydrates, fats, proteins) take place slowly not to overwhelm the mitochondria. However, our foods today are mostly stripped of fiber. Hence, sugars, fats, and proteins are hyper-absorbed and tend to reach the bloodstream and liver abruptly. This is worsened by the fact that our diet often comprises fructose. Unlike glucose which goes into the bloodstream, fructose aims directly for the liver. There, it is converted into fatty acid. The consequence of this is that fatty acid and glucose hit the mitochondria simultaneously even before the arrival of other components, thus jamming up the absorption process.

The Paradox of "Mono" Diets

Gundry maintains that the "balanced diets" usually prescribed by nutritionists rather cause weight gain and energy loss to create the perfect condition for the mitochondria. More extreme eating patterns like the Atkins diet, keto diet, duke rice diet, Okinawan diet, etc. They have been proven to make things easy for the mitochondria.

These kinds of diets, known as *mono diets*, contain limited fuel substrate (confined to one type of food. i.e., carbohydrate alone, fat alone, etc.) and make it easy to eat predictably. However, these eating patterns are only applicable in the short-term as it is almost impossible to keep up with them in the long term. While it is not advisable to follow these diets long-term, one can learn from them (to not overburden the mitochondria).

Mitochondrial Gridlock: A Recipe for Exhaustion

One of the causes of some people's energy loss is that they have lost their mitochondrial capacity to manufacture energy properly. This, in part, is because they are insulin resistant. Insulin resistance is the inability to burn sugar properly or use fatty acids as fuel. Hence, patients with insulin resistance are unable to gain from exercises.

The fact that many folks in this predicament feed on "balanced" diets raises some questions. This condition owes to the "gridlock" that stems from the bombardment of the mitochondria, thus slowing down the energy production process. The excessive energy that gets clogged up thus gets shuttled into fat cells (to burn them into energy again later).

Due to the energy "gridlock" and the overstuffing of fat cells that result from it, the mitochondria defend themselves against being overwhelmed. It does this by creating waxy lipids—*ceramides*—to strengthen and thicken the fat cells to prevent them from bursting as the fat content increases. When this happens, the ceramide slows down the fat absorption. Now, here is where insulin comes in. Insulin, made by the pancreas, is responsible for moving sugar and protein into the cells from the bloodstream with insulin receptors in the cell. However, with the presence of ceramides, this becomes difficult. This is because the ceramides block the ability of the insulin receptors to detect insulin outside the cell.

At this point, when one keeps eating foods that keep entering their bloodstream. The pancreas creates even more insulin (as a way of signaling louder to the cells to "open their doors" to let the proteins and sugar out of the bloodstream). Yet, more ceramide is released to deny them access. This is what results in insulin resistance. The basic solution to mitochondrial dysfunction is to eat less. This, like other diet solutions, doesn't address the problem permanently. Solution Action Plan available in Part 2.

One would feel unenergetic because the brain, like the rest of their body, is going through inflammation. It is likely "overfed and underpowered" (discussed already) and struggling to meet its energy needs. Over the years, symptoms such as foggy brain, muddied thinking, etc., which used to be suffered by only the elderly, have been linked with men and women in their thirties, forties, or younger. These symptoms can be accompanied by higher stress and anxiety levels, poor mood, or trouble falling asleep. The chances are that anyone experiencing a sudden loss of energy may be closing up on these cognitive symptoms.

Lack of energy plagues the whole body, including the brain. However, just as it is difficult to diagnose bodily fatigue, most physicians cannot diagnose mental weakness. Hence, relevant symptoms are usually dismissed. One of these is the lack of test patterns to diagnose neurological inflammation. However, there are new test markers for detecting brain inflammation. These have shown that cases of the leaky gut resulting in inflammation are also connected to *leaky brain*. A leaky brain is a condition in which the *blood-brain barrier* is compromised by inflammatory agents, thus leading to brain inflammation.

The brain is one of the most power-hungry organs in the body. Thinking, processing, and other neurological function consume up to twenty percent of the body's ATP production. It uses up to 13 pounds of ATP daily, which is five times its original weight. This explains why it is packed with mitochondria. With this in mind, it is important not to be dismissive of brain fogs; this can degenerate into more serious cognitive impairments (like Alzheimer's and Parkinson's disease) later in life. This is why it is important to turn around brain fog earlier in life.

The Second Brain

It is a common saying that **the gut is the second brain**. Gundry flips this perspective to argue that the gut itself is the first brain and that the grey matter in the head is only the second brain. This is because the brain is controlled from the gut; the gut has more to do with how one thinks, feels, and acts than the brain. However, they influence each other and communicate via a complex network known as the gut-brain axis. This network, upon recent studies, is now known as the *microbiota*-gut-brain axis.

While the gut is home to seventy to eighty percent of one's immune cells, it also houses over one hundred million neurons. These neurons, among other functions, help control digestion; more importantly, they receive and transmit information from the microbiome to the "big brain" in the head. They are a part of the *enteric nervous system*.

True to the connection of the gut and the brain, research links emotional stress and depression to digestive disorders. Stress can influence the environment in the intestines. Conversely, imbalances in the intestines can send signals to the brain, which may alter the mood. Research has shown that reintroducing helpful gut bacteria in the form of multispecies probiotics can cure sadness.

Depression and brain fog have been linked to changes in the gut biome. In the same vein, cognitive decline and dementia are influenced by leaky gut and abnormal microbiome. More and more studies have linked neurological or psychological issues to disturbances in the gut. Hence, they can be prevented or reversed by healing the gut and microbiome, which influences the brain.

How the Brain Becomes Inflamed

The vagus nerve is a nerve that starts at the brain and connects it to the heart and gut. It is the nerve you assess anytime you take deep, long breaths to calm yourself. It plays a key role in the connection of the brain and the microbiome. It is also involved in several regulatory activities such as regulating hunger and satisfaction levels, modulating inflammation, and monitoring energy needs. It picks and sends signals from the gut and sends them to the brain through some newly discovered cells known as *neuropods*. These cells detect can detect a leaky gut. When this happens, they send signals to the brain, causing the immune system to respond, thus triggering an inflammation.

Apart from the vagus nerve, another means of communication are free-floating inflammatory cytokines. Cytokines are triggered into the bloodstream through a leaky gut. They can cause some trouble by going through important barriers in the body. For instance, we have the blood-brain barrier, which protects the brain from dangerous elements and only supplies it with required materials like oxygen, amino acid, glucose, hormones, and water.

However, just like the walls in the intestines, this barrier is susceptible to environmental and dietary assaults. For instance, the Western diet, which is high in sugar and saturated fat but low in fiber, can weaken the strength of the blood-brain barrier, thus impairing cognitive and memory functions. Other materials that can weaken the blood-brain barrier are lectins and glyphosate (found in herbicides). P-glycoproteins or aquaporins, which are a class of lectins, can also weaken the blood-brain barrier. They are found in corn, soybeans, spinach, green bell peppers, potatoes, and tobacco. However, most of us may not react to these foods. Nevertheless, getting rid of them can make a difference in patients with leaky gut.

Recognizing the disruptions to the blood-brain barrier can help curb the epidemic of neurological challenges in societies today. Getting rid of harmful materials and chemicals in your diet can help protect your blood-brain barrier, prevent brain inflammation, and promote brain health. This would help prevent issues like depression, Alzheimer's, schizophrenia, etc.

Brain Neurons Cut From Supplies

Just like the gut, the brain has several neurons, which are cells that contribute to thinking. Their cell bodies have long branches known as *axons*, which, in turn, have even more branches—*dendrites*. These dendrites are far-reaching in all directions towards the dendrites shooting from the axons of other neurons. These ensure the connections of neurons via chemical signals passed between them. When this repeatedly happens between specific neurons, thoughts and memories are formed. The brain also has *microglia*, a set of immune cells that help protect it, get rid of dead cells, and fight off harmful invaders.

When the microglia learn from the vagus nerve that cytokines are attempting to get in via the bloodstream, they intensify their "cleansing" activities. They also help preserve the neurons they surround. At this point, the dendrites withdraw their extensions, thus making the neurons unable to communicate. In addition to this, the microglia prunes the axon sheaths. While this is a defensive action, it can be disastrous if it happens for a long period. It all springs from gut inflammation. Now, this pruning is responsible for the mentally impaired feeling one gets when sleep-deprived. Simple carbs and sugar-rich foods, which one turns to when sleep-deprived, also worsens the issue.

The microglia would only withdraw its defensive activities only when stress dies down, and anti-inflammatory signals are passed from the gut buddies. When this happens, it returns to simply protecting the brain. However, this wouldn't happen unless your brain has access to anti-inflammatory compounds anti-inflammatory gasotransmitters like hydrogen sulfide and hydrogen. However, in contemporary times, these anti-inflammatory compounds we require are mostly lacking in our roots and soils. In addition to this, the stress is chronic and ongoing. This reality is even further exacerbated by the fact that many consume high-sugar diets, which reduces the population of anti-inflammatory bugs.

Besides neuroinflammation (inflammation in the brain), the brain can also be disturbed by mitochondrial jam (or gridlock) discussed in chapter 4. An overwhelmed mitochondrion has also been linked to losing mental sharpness. Just as other body cells protect themselves by becoming insulin-resistant (explained in chapter 4), the neurons in the brain can also be blocked from insulin, thus starving the brain of glucose. This starves the brain of energy and causes inflammation. There are ways to retain or restore the brain's insulin sensitivity. This will be comprehensively discussed in part 2. However, they are based on four goals which are:

- Easing the load on the mitochondria via timed eating

- Eliminating foods that flood your system with sugar

- Taking food that inhibits ceramide production (olive oil, sesame oil, walnut, etc.)

- Feeding the gut buddies towards maintaining insulin sensitivity.

The previous chapters have introduced the first half of the formula, "E=M2C2," introduced at the start of the book. The two Ms, which represent microbe and mitochondria, have been examined thus far. We have thus learned that energy is dependent on the microbiome (gut buddies) and well-functioning mitochondria. Now, the C part of the formula is the most practical yet the most challenging.

Gundry recounts that his experience with one of his patients, "Big Ed," transformed his life. By simply changing their diet, Big Ed could reverse his severe inoperable coronary artery disease, regain insulin sensitivity, and recover his mental clarity. Influenced by this, Gundry experimented on himself by practicing Yale University dietary thesis on the early human diet. This worked for him, as he was able to lose seventy pounds in the process. When he started his Centers for Restorative Medicine to help patients reverse diseases with food supplements, he recommended changing the timing of meals.

As a practice, from January to June, Gundry restricts his eating window to two hours a day (staying twenty-two hours off eating). He notes that this time aligns with nature when there is less food (less food during winter and spring; more food during summer and fall). He increases his eating hours for the next six months to six to eight hours (staying sixteen to eighteen hours off food). He calls this practice *time-restricted eating*.

The practice of going without food for a longer period, for Gundry, can help increase energy levels. He argues that discomfort makes one stronger. This idea is built because plants that grow in mild but stressful conditions tend not to wither as expected. This is known as *hormesis*. Rather, they produce higher protective compounds that boost their health and make them nutritious to us too. Like in plants, hormesis works in all living things to prepare their cells to face hard times. Now, time-restricted eating doesn't mean eating less or consuming fewer calories; it only means restricting the time those calories are consumed.

Our bodies are designed to thrive with just the stress. This means we need some level of biological and environmental stressors. In line with this fact, studies have revealed several benefits of fasting, cold therapy, heat therapy, etc. These mild stressors clean up our cells, causing them to repair and restore themselves, thus helping to calm any inflammation. Fasting alone can aid DNA repair, increased antioxidant activities, boosted mitochondrial functions, anti-inflammation, etc. Again, fasting in this context is not to stop eating but to consciously time when you eat. It also features paying attention to the things you eat during your eating times or periods. Gundry calls this *Chrono Consumption*. Chrono consumption, for him, basically helps to maintain internal health, increasing the population of new bacteria, resetting the circadian clock in each of the cells, and boosting the genes that aid health. It also regulates the fuels you give to our mitochondria and minimizes the time they have to work to provide energy for you. This makes them efficient in providing you with energy.

Fasting is generically used to describe *intermittent fasting* and *time-restricted eating*. While these two kinds of fasting are often used interchangeably, they differ in the nutritional perspective. Intermittent fasting refers to water-only or low-calorie fasting for a twenty-four-hour period followed by normal eating for one or two days. It can also be applied every week (fasting for one week and going on normal feeding for another week or two). While this fasting method may aid weight loss and probably enhance longevity, it isn't as effective as time-restricted eating combined with feeding on foods with single fuel types or mono diets.

Mono diets, as already discussed in chapter 4, are restricted to only one type of food. They are thus useful for eliminating mitochondrial traffic jam which is often caused by consuming different fuel sources. While mono eating is not advisable for a long time (in the author's perspective), it is highly effective when combined with time-restricted eating. The hybrid plan of time-restricted eating and mono meals makes up the C2 part of Gundry's formula, E=M2C2.

Some research carried out on mice showed that full-calorie time-restricted eaters fared better all-day eaters, irrespective of whether their diet was high in fat, sucrose, etc. This is because the amount of time spent without eating prevented the mitochondria from being stuck. Another recent Italian study also showed that time-restricted eating enhanced health, weight loss, and protection against disease. Those who ate all day didn't get the same results despite eating the same number of calories as the time-restricted eaters.

Gundry argues against the conventional nutritional mainstay of "three square meals a day" and the studies that argue that breakfast is the most important meal. These perspectives, for him, hold no water in the evolutionary perspective. Our ancestors were unlikely to have practiced this method of eating. Besides, our hormonal operating system is designed to find breakfast strange. Our bodies are designed to get going every morning, irrespective of whether or not we have eaten.

Every morning, the adrenal glands flood the bloodstream with cortisol and epinephrine, causing the liver to make glucose available. This happens even after a prolonged period of staying off food. This aligns with the evolutionary fact that our ancestors lacked food storage systems and thus had to work and expend energy to fetch their food and ate most of it immediately. Another fact to note is that digestion takes a lot of energy. This is why research suggests that athletes fare better while in a fasted state.

Time-Controlled Eating Resets Your Body Clocks

Regular activities program the body according to a schedule. Changes between light and darkness, for instance, tilt the body's circadian clock, thus activating and deactivating genes. Just like plants, humans are designed to live by the natural cycle. This explains why one feels sleepy at night, feels awake at daytime, etc. In the same vein, eating patterns also tilt the clocks in our bodies to influence our energy and total health.

Now, all cells in our bodies have their clocks and are responsive to the changes from our fasting and eating periods. These clocks are aware of when we eat and when not to. Hence, any alteration that may occur from processing or digesting food for too long may signal a wrong time response in them, thus switching off the energy systems our bodies require to function effectively.

From evolution, we had a schedule of eating predictably, in sunlight, and not eating when it gets dark. During summer, we ate more due to the longer periods of light for hunting and gathering food, while, in winter, we ate for shorter periods (due to shorter periods of light).

Our circadian clocks were wired after this pattern. And we get the most from our bodies when we eat in line with it.

In line with our evolutionary eating patterns, studies carried out on Muslim groups have revealed that Ramadan fasts (which entails eating just after sunset and before sunrise for thirty days) have long-term and short-term health benefits. The research showed that protective genes were turned on while cancerous genes were switched off. The "fasting" also helped boost proteins which helped protect against neuron damage, metabolize sugar, and regulate insulin.

Another study, by Dr. Satchin Panda of Salk Institute, carried out on human volunteers showed that reducing one's eating hours to ten (at most) while staying off food for fourteen hours (at least) is highly beneficial as it helped improve energy, sleep, mood, and thinking in just a few months. It also helped overweight people lose weight.

The Optimal Eating Window

Gundry prescribes, as a general rule, eating daily meals in no more than twelve hours. Six to eight hours is ideal. He maintains that, even though this could be difficult for most persons, it can be practiced and developed gradually. You may not have to start eating only six hours a day (eighty percent of persons would struggle with this). Most people who are insulin-resistant would suffer physical exhaustion the moment their body runs out of glucose. This is because they don't have the metabolic flexibility to convert free fatty acid to energy. All sorts of physical discomfort suffered make most people give up on this. Part 2 presents gradual steps to help practice this eating method towards regaining energy.

Move It to Boost It

Another important point to note about Chrono Consumption is that exercise can boost the physical benefits of fasting. Exercise teaches one's cells to be tough and to be able to deal with unforeseen difficult situations. As metabolic organs, the muscles absorb sugar and fat-storing them as glycogen for later use. However, exercise depletes this glycogen in the muscles to a point where it burns the free fatty acids faster. This improves one's metabolic flexibility. It also aids in the secretion of *myokines*, a chemical that improves insulin sensitivity, regulates hormones, and facilitates brain health. However, eating before exercising may impede these benefits.

Another reason why exercises may not be beneficial to some is their gut microbiome. This is the case with patients with type 2 diabetes. While those with a healthy gut microbiome may become insulin-sensitive and lose weight from exercising, those without a healthy or balanced microbiome wouldn't experience notable changes.

Seven Deadly Energy Disruptors

Before going into Gundry's energy paradox program (to help address energy challenges or practically), here are troubling external factors/energy disruptors he presents as responsible for energy challenges. These disruptors are the unsuitable foods, chemicals, and other toxic environmental influences we encounter daily. They pose a threat to one's intestinal and microbiome health. When exposed to these disruptors, they can weaken the gut wall and reduce the population of the healthy gut microbiome, thus causing an imbalance in the gut ecosystem. The result of all these is inflammation, which, in turn, culminates in constant depletion of one's energy or damage of the mitochondria. Here are the disruptors

Disruptor 1: Antibiotics

Americans have eight million pounds of antibiotics annually prescribed in the medical system. The food system exposes us to antibiotics even further, like five times this amount is given to animals to boost their growth. The kind of antibiotics we are exposed to is the *broad-spectrum antibiotics*, which works by killing all strains of bacteria simultaneously. Even though they were intended to and are capable of countering life-threatening infections, they are constantly being used for milder situations where they aren't required. This is not without several health consequences like obesity, autoimmune disorders, depression, fatigue, etc.

What broad-spectrum antibiotics do is fight the whole microbiome ecosystem (in a bid to get rid of invaders). This wipes out the bacterial diversity in the gut microbiome. It also affects the growth of immune cells, thus making one more vulnerable to pathogens. These antibiotics can also damage the mitochondria and eventually through oxidative stress. Overall, they can damage the energy system. Unfortunately, most Americans are regularly exposed to these antibiotics even if they aren't taking them in pill forms. They can be consumed in meats (from animals raised on them) and even plants.

Disruptor 2: Glyphosate (Roundup)

Roundup is the world's most widely used herbicide. Just like several others, its active ingredient is glyphosate. Glyphosate can best be understood as a version of antibiotics meant for the earth. It simply kills plants by fighting the components in it. It is found in many of our foods and water today and is one of the most common disruptors as far as energy is concerned today. This is because it is now a widespread farming practice to use them as a desiccant to grow non-GMO crops like oats, corn, wheat, etc. It has been observed to loosen the intestinal walls and the blood-brain barrier, thus making room for invaders and resulting in inflammation. It is also dangerous to mitochondrial health.

Disruptor 3: Environmental Chemicals

We are constantly exposed to hundreds of harmful artificial chemicals today. Hundreds of thousands of these chemicals are constantly brought into our environment in different forms of consumer products. They thus dominate our air, water, soil, homes, workplaces, food, etc. Some common ones are plastic industry chemicals of different kinds, herbicides, pesticides, biocides, etc. These chemicals have been linked to all forms of poor health outcomes. These include the alteration of the gut microbiome, chronic liver and intestinal inflammation, and metabolic disorder.

Disrupter 4: Overused Pharmaceutical Drugs

The use of pharmaceutical drugs can be essential sometimes and can (and should) help you to a point where you can do without them. However, relying on them or using them for a long time can threaten one's energy systems. Like antibiotics, anti-inflammatory drugs like naproxen, ibuprofen, Voltaren, Celebrex, etc., also pose a threat to the gut microbiome. They can also damage the colon and small intestine barrier, thus making room for lectins to invade the system.

Proton pump inhibitors (PPIs) and other anti-blocking drugs like Zantac, Protonix, Nexium, etc., can be equally harmful. They are known to reduce stomach acid. In doing this, they can also reduce important stomach acid. This can result in the overgrowth of less-helpful microbes and can also culminate in inflammation. They can also affect proton pumps in all the body cells, thus slowing doesn't energy. When this happens to the cells in the brain, cognitive impairment, brain fog, and dementia show up.

Disrupter 5: Fructose

Fructose is the natural sugar found in honey, fruits, corn, some vegetables, etc. Even our natural diets (non-processed foods) and drinks are filled with fructose. Over time, our fruits have been engineered to be sweeter and higher in fructose to drive sales. Now, unlike glucose, fructose is absorbed from the intestines into the liver. While there, it prevents adenosine monophosphate from the ATP production chain in the mitochondria, causing it to produce uric acid, which is the cause of high blood pressure, kidney stones, etc. Fructose has also been linked to fatty liver disease, heart disease, etc.

Disruptor 6: Junk Light

While there has always been junk food, "junk lite" has recently been discovered. It is still being studied. But studies have already shown that light bulb poses a lot of health hazard. This is because artificial light disrupts our natural relationship with the sun and all life forms. This eventually alters one's circadian rhythm, thus affecting their metabolic functions. Constant excessive exposure to fluorescent lights, light from computer screens, etc., has been linked to increased stress levels. While you may be unable to escape junk light entirely, you can stay away from it as much as you can.

Disruptor 7: Electromagnetic Fields (EMFs)

This refers to the unseen human-made electromagnetic frequencies from the wireless communication networks all around us. They were made to transmit data to our electronic and mobile devices. Some people are highly sensitive to them and have experienced symptoms like fatigue, headaches, brain fog, etc. Every other person exposed to them is also affected in one way or another at cellular levels. Nevertheless, we can mitigate its effects on us by regulating the way we use our devices. (This will be comprehensively discussed in chapter 10).

Part 2: The Energy Paradox Program

Chapter 7: The Energy Paradox Eating Program

This part provides solutions to solving your energy-related problems towards restoring your get-up-and-go. This starts with the foods you eat and the ones you don't eat. This entails eating food that ensures the health of your microbiome and mitochondria and neglect foods that don't. Combining this with Chrono Consumption helps improve insulin sensitivity and enhance its metabolic flexibility. Three key objectives make up the Energy Paradox Program. They are:

- Heal your roots
- Regenerate the soil
- End mitochondrial gridlock

The program is flexible and wouldn't compel anyone to eat what they don't want to eat. It suits all categories of people, whether they are vegetarians or carnivores. All you would have to do is to eat in such a way that suits your gut microbiome (or gut buddies); this means giving them the kinds of foods they require. The program also features the use of ketones.

The Energy Paradox program emphasizes eating foods in their natural state as they can be. This means your diet should mostly consist of vegetables with prebiotic fiber, wild fish, nuts and seeds, omega-3 eggs, low-fructose fruits, grass-fed meat, poultry, etc. Dark chocolate, Champaign, or red wine may be fine for dessert. The prescribed food promises to be delicious; however, it'll be different from what you're used to.

Energy Paradox Program Food Rules

These are the guiding rules in the Energy Paradox eating program. It is designed to aid in repairing the gut wall towards revitalizing the gut wall and microbiome while also restoring metabolic flexibility and insulin sensitivity.

THE Dos

Rule 1: Eat Foods rich in prebiotic fiber

While it is great to take prebiotics, it is even better to eat foods that help feed the good bacteria in the gut. This entails eating food rich in probiotic fibers. When the healthy bacteria in the gut are well-fed with prebiotic fibers, they help nourish your mitochondria. Rutabagas, tubers, okra, asparagus, onions, leeks, flaxseeds, parsnips, radishes, pressure-cooked beans, legumes, etc., some foods rich in prebiotic fiber.

Rule 2: Eat foods that aid postbiotic production

This includes vegetables that contain sulfur. Some examples are broccoli, cauliflower, onions, shallot, leeks, garlic, chives, etc. They help gut bacteria prevent fatty liver disease and similar diseases.

Rule 3: Make your starches more resistant

Starches are "resistant" when they are processed more slowly in the small intestine. This helps to avoid mitochondrial gridlocks. Pressure-cooked rice, yams, millet, taro root, cassava, etc., can become resistant when cooked, frozen, and reheated.

Rule 4: Eat fruits only when in season; eat moderately

As has already been discussed, excessive fructose can pose trouble to the liver and cell mitochondria. Keeping fruit intake minimal can thus be very helpful.

Rule 5: Enjoy mitochondrial must-haves: Phospholipids and Melatonin

Melatonin and phospholipids are important to the health of the mitochondria as they help ensure their health and avoid oxidative stress. Pistachios, dark-colored rice, red rice mushrooms, olive oil, red wine, black pepper, mustard seeds, almonds, etc., are some examples of foods rich in melatonin. Shellfishes like oysters, shrimps, crabs, lobsters, clams, etc., are rich in phospholipids.

THE DON'Ts

While the top five rules provide you guidelines for the best foods to revitalize and restore your energy systems, the following are foods that can pose a threat to your energy and overall health.

Rule 6: Leave the Lectins

This means avoiding foods loaded with lectins. This includes foods like pseudo-grains (quinoa, amaranth, buckwheat, etc.), bread, white potatoes, beans, brown rice, peppers, corn, lentils, etc. White rice, red rice, and black rice have lower lectin loads which are acceptable when pressure-cooked. Foods loaded with lectins can be dangerous to one's energy systems and overall health because they are difficult to digest (and may cause digestive damage), cause holes in one's intestinal walls, and cause weight gain.

Rule 7: Stop the sugar

One of the challenges with our modern diet is that most of our foods contain carbohydrates and refined sugar. Most people are not aware of this. This is even worsened by the fact that many –food products' labels hide their sugar contents. Almost all prepackaged foods contain some high-fructose corn syrup. Hence it's smart to avoid any product with labels like "all-natural syrup," "brown rice syrup," "corn syrup," etc. Some other sweet alternatives to refined sugar will be listed later.

Rule 8: Use protein to restore flexibility, but don't overdo it

While protein can be used as a good source of calories, it is important to consume it minimally. This is because digesting protein takes a lot of energy—we spend 30 percent of the calories in them on digestion. Hence, protein-rich diets (modified Atkins diet, high carnivore diet, etc.) can result in the burning of protein calories. However, as an advantage, they limit the mitochondrial energy sources to one substrate, thus preventing gridlock. On the downside, this can starve the gut buddies of fiber and other needed nutrients. If one must eat animal protein, it has to minimal and should include wild fish, wild shellfish, omega-3 eggs, and other omega-3 rich foods.

Rule 9: Don't eat Frankenfoods loaded with Franken fats

The regular American diet is loaded with lots of fatty foods and processed sugar. This makes it very inflammatory and energy-draining. Particularly, it alters the gut microbiome and poses a threat to overall health. Avoiding diets high in fried foods containing trans-fat (corn oil, soybean oil, etc.) is key here. Foods prepared with olive oil and sesame oil are much healthier replacements.

It's Time for Chrono Consumption

With this knowledge of what to eat and what not to eat to keep the mitochondria and gut microbiome healthy, we can now apply Chrono Consumption. Combined with the right foods, it will help restore the body's natural circadian rhythms and limit the pressure on the mitochondria. Many may find this part difficult among the Energy Paradox program schedule, but it has been designed to make it easy for a newcomer. The Chrono Consumption plan is structured to begin with the regular twelve-hour eating window and gradually narrow it down to eight or six hours a day. You can choose to eat as you please on weekends.

Mono Your Way into the Day

While you restrict your eating window, it is important to give your mitochondria a break by only supplying them with one fuel source for the first meal. This is in line with the advantages of mono diets discussed in chapter 4. However, it isn't advisable to practice this for a longer period, hence the need to confine it to just the day's first meal. Given this, the first meal of the day will be an almost pure protein or almost pure carbohydrate.

You can opt for fonio prepared for carbohydrates like oatmeal, millet cereal with almond milk, prebiotic shake, etc. For protein, you can opt for scrambled egg whites, grass-fed animals, Canadian bacon, etc. Vegan alternatives for protein are basil seed pudding; protein powder shakes, etc. It is important to without pure fat meals till the third week as you may not have the metabolism to burn fat at the starting point. In the third week, you can bring them in.

The Energy Paradox program will last for six weeks. From Monday to Friday of every week, you'll delay your breakfast by one hour each day and take your last meal by 7 pm. For instance, if you have your first at 7 am on Monday, you'd have it at 8 am on Tuesday, 9 am on Wednesday, and so on till Friday. In the following week, you delay your breakfast one hour later than you had it the previous week. If you had your breakfast at 7 am on the first day (Monday) of the previous week, you will have your breakfast at 8 am in the current week. Throughout the new week, you continue delaying your breakfast by one hour per day. In the following week, you delay your breakfast by another one hour later than the previous week. However, all through, your breakfast wouldn't exceed noon. It'll look like this.

First Week— Monday (7 am), Tuesday (8 am), Wednesday (9 am), Thursday (10 am), Friday (11 am)

Second Week— Monday (8 am), Tuesday (9 am), Wednesday (10 am), Thursday (11 am), Friday (12 am)

Third Week— Monday (9 am), Tuesday (10 am), Wednesday (11 am), Thursday (12 am), Friday (12 am)

Fourth Week— Monday (10 am), Tuesday (11 am), Wednesday (12 am), Thursday (12 am), Friday (12 am)

Fifth Week— Monday (11 am), Tuesday (11 am), Wednesday (12 am), Thursday (12 am), Friday (12 am)

Sixth Week— Monday (12 am), Tuesday (12 am), Wednesday (12 am), Thursday (12 am), Friday (12 am)

The logic behind this system is to gradually train your body to adapt to the new routine. It is effective for conditioning your metabolism. The free weekend will provide a window for relaxation and preparation for the next week. By the end of the six weeks of carefully following up with this routine, you may find it pretty easy to practice it. What is important is that you don't go back to your old routine. This will help your microbiome and circadian rhythms settle effectively.

Don't Skip Out on Meal Skipping.

You are likely to get uncomfortably hungry when you first start this program. This may be particularly so in the first week, as you may find it difficult to delay your breakfast later and later. However, it is important that you embrace it and not panic about it. What is important here is that you stick to the program till you can reap results. This means setting new targets every time you compromise. If you find it difficult to make it to 9 am on the first Wednesday, for instance, you can stay at 8 am, or just a little over 8 am. You can then set a new target for yourself. You can take lots of prebiotic fibers to deal with hunger pangs.

Eat, Pause, and Eat

If, as the program progresses, you are unable to start your day without food, you can subscribe to Ramadan-styled fasting. Research shows that this style of fasting shares the same benefits as time-controlled eating. The fast gives a twelve-hour non-eating window during the day and an eight-hour non-eating window during the night. However, here, try opting for a mono breakfast, shelve lunch, and wait for dinner. This may equip you with the ability to start delaying breakfast.

The Energy Paradox Food Lists

This is the crux of the Energy Paradox program. This list should be considered complementary to the Dos and DONTs rules we earlier went through. (You can access more information and downloadable PDFs via www.drgundry.com)

Energy-Boosting Foods

Cruciferous Vegetables— arugula, Brussels sprouts, bok choy, broccoli, collards, cauliflower, cabbage (green and red), kimchee, kale, kohlrabi, watercress, swiss chard, radicchio, sauerkraut (raw), radicchio.

Other Vegetables— asparagus, artichokes, carrot greens, celery, bamboo shoots, beets (raw), carrots (raw), chicory, garlic, daikon radish, ginger, chives, fiddlehead ferns, garlic scapes, hearts of palm, horseradish, leeks, mushrooms, Jerusalem artichokes (sunchokes), lemongrass, nopales (cactus; available online), radishes, onions, okra, parsnips, rutabaga, puntarella, scallions, water chestnuts, shallots.

<u>Leafy Greens</u>— algae, spinach, butter lettuce, basil, cilantro, endive, dandelion greens, fennel, escarole, mint, parsley, mesclun (baby greens), mizuna, mustard greens, parsley, purslane, perilla, red and green leaf lettuces, romaine lettuce, seaweed, sea vegetables.

<u>Fruits that act like Fats</u>— all types of Olives, Avocado.

<u>Oils</u>— black seed oil, algae oil (Thrive culinary brand), organic and non-GMO canola oil, avocado oil, coconut oil, MCT oil, extra virgin olive oil, cod liver oil, macadamia oil, rice bran oil, perilla oil, pistachio oil, plain and toasted sesame oil, red palm oil, rice bran oil, walnut oil.

<u>Nuts and Seeds (half cup a day)</u> — brazil nuts (in limited amount), almonds (only blanched or Marcona), chestnuts, barùkas nuts, coconut, coconut milk (unsweetened), flaxseeds, hemp seeds, macadamia nuts, pecans, hazelnuts, hemp protein powder, milkadamia creamer (unsweetened), pili nuts, pistachios, pine nuts, sesame seeds, nut butter, psyllium seeds, tahini, walnuts, Sacha Inchi seeds.

<u>*Resistant Starches (eat moderately)*</u> — green bananas, green mango, baobab tree, celery root, green plantains, green papayas, cassava, jicama, parsnips, rutabaga, tiger nuts, sweet potatoes/yams, millet, persimmon, sorghum, taro root, turnips, yucca.

<u>Acceptable Noodles</u>— Slim pasta, cassava pasta, Edison Grainery, sorghum pasta, Kanten Pasta, Jovial cassava pasta, GundryMD's Pasta, kelp noodles, miracle noodles, konjac noodles, millet pasta, shirataki noodles, miracle rice.

<u>Seafood (four ounces a day)</u> — Alaskan salmon, clams, halibut, lobster, anchovies, crab, calamari/squid, mussels, scallops, sardines, scallops, freshwater bass, halibut, tuna, oysters, whitefish, Hawaiian fish,

<u>Pastured Poultry (four ounces a day)</u> — goose, duck, chicken, ostrich, turkey, omega-3 eggs.

<u>Grass-fed Meat (four ounces a day)</u> — bison, elk, beef, boar, lamb, venison, pork, wild game.

Fruits in season (small servings per weekend) — apples, blackberries, apricots, blueberries, kiwis, cherries, crispy pears, nectarines, pomegranates, plums, passion fruit, strawberries, peaches.

Herbs, condiments, and seasonings— coconut aminos, avocado mayonnaise, mustard, miso, fish sauce (no sugar added), herbs and spices, sea salt, vanilla extract, nutritional yeast, sea salt, tahini, wasabi, vinegar.

Flours— almond (blanched), cassava, chestnut, arrowroot, grape seed, coffee fruit, coconut, millet, green banana, hazelnut, sesame (and seeds), tiger nut, sorghum flour, sweet potato.

Beverages— red wine, hydrogen water, champagne, coffee, all types of tea, dark spirits.

Lectin-Containing Foods to Avoid

Refined Starchy Foods— bread, crackers, cereal, pastries, rice, wheat flour, cookies, pasta, potato chips, potatoes, rice, tortillas.

Grains, Pseudo Grains, and Grasses— barley, buckwheat, brown rice, barley grass, bulgur, einkorn, corn, corn products, corn syrup, Kamut, popcorn, oats, einkorn, kasha, quinoa, rye, wheat, wheatgrass, white rice (except pressure-cooked), wild rice.

Sugar and Sweeteners— diet drinks, agave, granulated sugar, coconut sugar, maltodextrin, Splenda (sucralose), NutraSweet (aspartame), acesulfame-K, sweet'n Low (saccharin).

Vegetables— beans* (including sprouts), edamame, green beans, legumes, sugar snap peas, chickpeas (including hummus), lentils, pea protein, soy, peas.

Nuts and Seeds— cashew, almonds with peels, peanuts, sunflower seeds, pumpkin seeds, chia seeds.

Fruits (called vegetables) — tomatoes, chiles, bell peppers, cucumbers, any kind of melons, squash, goji berries, eggplant, pumpkin, squash (any kind), zucchini, tomatillos.

Milk Products Containing A1 Casein— ice cream, milk, butter, cheese, frozen yogurt, cottage cheese, ricotta, kefir.

<u>Oils</u>— canola (most is GMO), grape-seed, corn, peanut, cottonseed, partially hydrogenated oils, safflower, soy, vegetable, sunflower.

<u>Herbs and Seasoning</u>— red chile flakes, soy sauce, ketchup, mayonnaise (except avocado mayonnaise), soy sauce, steak sauce, Worcestershire sauce.

Here you go! This furnishes you with sufficient information for nourishing your gut buddies towards keeping you energetic and healthy.

The modern innovations in the world (cars, air conditioners) have made life so easy for us. However, they make things harder for our bodies. This is because the human body is designed to endure and thrive in physical challenges. We require some level of environmental and biological stress to stay healthy. The choices we make daily can either boost or drain our energy. Gundry thus projects important lifestyle factors to stay healthy. These are the "Six Ss." They are Sweat, Sunlight, Shutdown Mode, Sleep, Sensory Challenges, and Stress Management. These are discussed in the following paragraphs.

Sweat: It takes Energy to Sweat

Our bodies are naturally wired for movement. This explains one of the fundamental reasons why the Hadzas' hunter-gatherers are healthier than the regular American office worker. Their hunter-gatherer lifestyle is naturally physically demanding. They squat or sit on their hunches instead of just sitting comfortably. This exercises the muscles in the backs of their legs and makes it easy for them to get up and down as many times as possible.

The modern idea of fitness is linked to some few minutes of activity (exercise), while the bulk of the time is spent without physical activity. However, if, like the Hadzas and other hunter-gatherer ancestors, we spend a lot of time moving, standing, etc., we will be able to burn glucose stored as glycogen, help our mitochondria burn fatty acids, and help maintain overall health.

Now, in exercising, you don't need to spend too much of your time all at once. You can practice *exercise snacking*. This means scattering three to ten minutes of exercises throughout the whole day. The goal here is to continue to stay active throughout the whole day. Studies have linked exercise snacking with increased metabolism, increased energy production, improved mental clarity, and decreased blood sugar. Some exercise routines you can practice through the whole day are squats, crunches, planks, etc.

Sunlight: Nature's Free Vitamin

Exposure to sunlight supplies the body with vitamin D, which has been found to support the intestinal walls and immune systems, thus increasing energy production. The sun also plays a key role in our energy production by supplying us with full-spectrum natural light, which gives our skin melanin while also helping our bodies produce Adenosine Triphosphate (ATP). The light that comes from the sun has also been linked to lower blood pressure, easy blood flow, improved mood, and sleep. Regular sun exposure is thus important to energy production and overall health.

Shutdown Mode: Turn off the Blue Light

As has already been discussed in chapter 6, the sun programs our internal clock, regulating how we sleep and eat. In the absence of electricity, our ancestors slept and ate according to regular changes in sunlight exposure. Constant exposure to sunlight programmed their circadian clock, thus providing a natural rhythm for eating and sleeping. This helped them eat and sleep most healthily.

However, the invention of electricity and artificial light (junk light) altered this in humans. The natural rhythm which made humans eat and sleep healthily is thus exchanged for an unhealthy artificial pattern. Over time, junk light has been found to have altered our circadian clocks, disrupting our natural sleep patterns. Given the realities of our times, junk light is difficult to escape (the light from electric bulbs, electronic devices, etc.). Nevertheless, we can stay away from artificial lights or "junk lights" as much as possible.

Sleep: Recharging Our Cells

As a nation, we have become accustomed to being sleep-deprived. But this can be harmful to overall health. Restful sleep impacts our health in so many ways. Getting restful sleep will mean getting rid of obstacles. Blue light (junk light), for instance, has been found to disrupt sleep patterns by altering one's circadian clock. It is also important to eat a minimum of three hours before going to bed. This is because digestion can divert the blood flow required for the brain to carry out its refreshing and self-cleansing works (necessary during sleep), thus preventing sleep. If you usually don't find it easy to fall asleep, engage more in exercises during the day. An active day and a restful night go hand-in-hand.

Sensory Challenges: When Too Much of a Hard Thing Is a Good Thing

Hard things like exercises and time-restricted eating (as have already been discussed) serve as sources of beneficial stress to the body. Exposure to the sun or cold, for instance, has been found to have beneficial reactions to the energy systems and overall health.

Stress Management: Chill Out to Power Up

In the past, stress invaded our lives in short bursts, providing sufficient time for rest and recovery. However, in modern times, stress is persistent and continuous. This increases inflammation and poses a threat to the health of the gut and our energy. Reclaiming our energy would mean staying off these high levels of stress. This requires two nonnegotiable practices: daily exercises (enhancing sound sleep and reducing stress) and controlled breathing (taking deep conscious breaths to access your vagus nerve, calm your nervous system, and communicating with your gut buddies). Besides controlled breathing, consciously practicing gratitude and meditation. These have also been linked with improved gut help.

This chapter presents a batch of recipes that are ideal for the health of your mitochondria and gut microbiome. The recipes have to be combined with Chrono Consumption for great effectiveness (as already discussed in previous chapters). You can modify any of these recipes to serve as the first meal of the day (as close as possible to a mono meal). It begins with a five-day meal plan for the first week of the Energy Paradox program.

Simple Meal Plan

<u>Day 1</u>

Breakfast— millet cereal with unsweetened almond milk

Lunch— Mushroom soup

Dinner— Kate's Thanksgiving Salad

<u>Day 2</u>

Breakfast— Fonio (millet), sorghum, or millet "oatmeal" with unsweetened almond milk

Lunch— Kale, Broccoli, and Millet Burger with Creamy Avocado Sauce

Dinner— Lectin-Free Fried Oysters and "Banh Mi" Bowl

<u>Day 3</u>

Breakfast— four scrambled egg whites with herbs of your choice

Lunch— Ground "Beef" Tacos

Dinner— Spanish-Style Shellfish Stew

<u>Day 4</u>

Breakfast— Hemp Green Protein Smoothie

Lunch— Almost-Classic Clam Chowder

Dinner— Mushroom and Shellfish Coconut Curry

<u>Day 5</u>

Breakfast— Cauliflower Waffles (the mono meal version)

Lunch— Instant Pot Lentil, Kale, Leek, and Mushroom Soup

Dinner— Cauliflower Risotto with Scallops

Overreliance on supplements to eliminate brain fog, sluggishness, and fatigue can be harmful as they do not help address the root challenges. However, when combined with a healthy diet and lifestyle, they can help promote energy. The following supplements will help reduce inflammation, nourish a healthy gut microbiome, and promote energy if effectively combined with the Energy Paradox program discussed in the book thus far.

Magnesium

Magnesium has been linked to several benefits. This includes improving sleep, easing muscle pain, strengthening metabolic health, etc. It does this by influencing insulin to help from the bloodstream into muscle cells where it should be. This also helps reverse insulin resistance. 299mg of magnesium with 99mg of potassium twice a day may just be fine. If you experience diarrhea from taking magnesium,

Glycine

Glycine can help protect the gut against the effects of glyphosate. It has also been found to aid sleep and maintain body temperature. For improved sleep, take 1009mg of glycine before bed. Against the effects of glyphosate, 200mg a day is okay.

Vitamin K2

Vitamin K2 is a key mineral missing in our modern diets. Grass-fed milk products are a good source of it. You can opt for it directly in supplements. 100 mcg daily dosage is fine.

Energy B Vitamins (Methyl B12, Vitamin B6, and Methyl Folate)

The author recommends daily supplements of B vitamins. 1000 to 5000mcb of Methyl B12 under the tongue, 1000mcg of Methyl Folate, and 50 to 100mg of Vitamin B6.

Liver Protectors

This can be effective in protecting one from fatty liver disease. The author recommends a daily 100mg dose for polyphenol milk thistle and a component of orange peel called d-limonene.

Berberine and Quercetin

Berberine is found in plants like Oregon grape roots and bayberry. And Quercetin is found in onions, apples, and citrus fruits. They have both been associated with mitochondrial repair. The author recommends 500mg of both twice daily.

Ketone Salts

They are ideal for the production of ketones. They are available in powders and capsules. The author recommends a dose of 10,000mg mixed ketone salts early in the morning.

The Energy Paradox G8

This refers to the nutrients recommended by the author as such that should be incorporated into every diet to promote gut health, overall health, and longevity. They comprise eight supplements (an addition to the seven nutrients, known as G7, which the author had recommended in his previous Paradox book series).

Vitamin D3: many patients with exhaustion, metabolic inflexibility, and autoimmune conditions are in that state because they are deficient in Vitamin D3. The author recommends taking 100–150mg/ml of Vitamin D supplements. Besides, regular exposure to the sun is also a great source of vitamin D.

Polyphenols: Polyphenols are natural energy boosters. They are good for the heart, healing, improvement of blood vessel functions, etc. Fruits like mulberries, pomegranate, Aronia berries, and dragon fruit are rich sources of polyphenols. Extra virgin olive oil, flax seeds, red wine, ginger, kale, endive, tea, etc., are also rich sources.

Green Plant Phytochemicals: The author recommends taking this to help reduce the cravings for unhealthy food like fats and simple sugars. He prescribes a combination of spinach extract with other greens like diindolylmethane (DIM). 500mg of spinach extract (which is available in capsules) twice a day is just fine. 100mg of Dim once a day is equally effective.

Prebiotics: This has already been discussed in Part 1. Specific supplements like ground flaxseeds and psyllium powder are great sources. A teaspoon of any of these a day is sufficient to give one's day a lift.

Lectin Blockers: While it's difficult always to avoid lectins, some compounds can serve as a shield against them. You use them by taking two capsules of lectin blockers before a lectin-filled meal. Examples of these supplements are Move Free and Osteo Bi-Flex.

Sugar Defenses: Since many of our meals contain simple sugars and pose a threat to metabolic conditions and insulin resistance. While you minimize sugar to the best of your ability, supplements containing selenium, zinc, turmeric extract, berberine, and black pepper extracts can cushion its effect too.

Long-Chain Omega-3s: Studies have linked the presence of omega-3 fats in the blood to better memory, cognition, and a bigger brain. A once-a-day tablespoon of fish oil supplements like Nature's Bounty, OmegaVia, Carlson cod liver oil, or Carlson Elite Gems can be just effective. 1000mg of DHA or EPA once a day can be just fine.

Mitochondrial Boosters: While exposure to sunlight and mitochondria are some of the surest ways of maintaining the health of your mitochondria, some compounds can also contribute to it. A few are 500mg of N-acetyl L-cysteine (NAC), 450mg of gynostemma extract, 300mg of shilajit, 50mg of pau d'arco, and 150mg of reduced or L-glutathione.

Discussion Questions

- What is inflammation?

- What are the factors that may trigger inflammation? And why?

- What are the effects of inflammation on the body's energy systems?

- Why has traditional medicine been unable to effectively deal with energy loss?

- What are the fundamental lifestyle differences between the Hadzas and the average modern American?

- What is responsible for the Hadzas' healthier and more energetic life?

- What is leaky gut? What triggers it?

- What are Lectins? What danger o do they pose to the body's energy systems?

- What are gut buddies? What is their value to the body's energy systems?

- What is the value of the body's mitochondria to the energy system?

- What's the cause of insulin resistance and how can it be effectively addressed?

- Why is the gut described as the second brain?

- How does the brain become inflamed? What are its effects? How can it be effectively addressed?

- What does **E=M2C2** stand for?

- Explain the application of **E=M2C2** in the promotion of energy and overall health.

- What lifestyle changes are you resorting to as a result of this book? (Write them down and work with them).

- What are your action plans for inculcating your new plans for a healthy lifestyle henceforth?

Thank you for choosing this book! If you enjoyed reading, please support us by giving us your five-star ratings/reviews. You may also like to get these other related book summaries from us:

Made in the USA
Monee, IL
22 December 2023

50411855R00031